GW00492673

JOHN
BRADBURNE
Soldier, poet, pilgrim

JOHN BRADBURNE

Soldier, poet, pilgrim

Fr Gerard Skinner

All booklets are published
thanks to the generosity of the supporters
of the Catholic Truth Society

All rights reserved. First published 2023 by The Incorporated Catholic Truth Society, 42-46 Harleyford Road, London SE11 5AY. Tel: 020 7640 0042 © 2023 The Incorporated Catholic Truth Society. www.ctsbooks.org

ISBN 978 1 78469 752 5

CONTENTS

The Way of a Pilgrim

John Bradburne's pilgrimage of life took him from the hills of Lancashire to a leper camp in Africa. The path that he followed had so many twists and turns that no one could have predicted where he would ultimately find and live his God-given vocation. It seems that many of those whose lives he touched were aware that John Bradburne was, at the very least, different. A visitor to the leper camp at Mtemwa, where Bradburne dedicated the latter part of his life, recalled: "The love of God shone through John Bradburne." A priest visiting Mtemwa reflected:

> He impressed me as being very ascetic, and this marked me. Was he eccentric? He was eccentric in the sense that

he was unusual, quite different from others in his way of life. His simplicity, joy, openness, and friendliness made us reflect on our attitudes and way of life.

His most remarkable trait was that he was truly human, immensely human. There was something very beautiful in this quality of humanity that he had. He laughed at himself, he refused to take himself seriously, but at the same time I felt that he must have struggled long to become what he truly was: himself.

His great quality, which I have also felt in the presence of other holy people, was that in his company you felt good. He was neither frivolous nor hail-fellow-well-met, but quite simply positive, affirmative, interested in you for what you were, what you had to say, what you did.

Zimbabwe's war of independence slowly encircled John Bradburne and claimed his friends' lives. Yet he remained with his 'family' of lepers, remarking in his usual self-deprecating way, "but would they waste a bullet on a clown?"

CHAPTER 1

Early Years

Cradled in the folding land beneath Cross Fell, one of England's highest mountains, lies the Cumbrian village of Skirwith. There, in the vicarage, on 14th June 1921, John Bradburne was born. He was the third son of the Reverend Thomas Bradburne and his wife, Erica. The newborn was named after the dedication of the village church, a High Anglican church in which he was baptised John Randal Bradburne on 31st July 1921.

The Bradburne family were blessed with a decently sized vicarage with a large garden. The garden gave Thomas Bradburne ample opportunity to grow vegetables and breed chickens. Flowerbeds and trees framed an extensive lawn.

This was the setting in which John Bradburne spent his earliest years.

By all accounts he was full of energy, indeed somewhat hyperactive and accident-prone and also possessed musical talent, greatly enjoying singing and acquiring some skill playing the harmonium. He enjoyed hearing the stories that his mother would read to him each day after lunch: Kipling, Beatrix Potter, the Brothers Grimm, Shakespeare and Dickens all playing a part in forming the young man's imagination. According to his sister, Mary, the young John was absent-minded and carefree: "The term 'free spirit' was never more appropriate to anyone than to John." She later recalled: "He was never 'run of the mill'. And he devoted himself to things like home-life, birds, pets and adventurous undertakings." All this was combined with a passionate and sensitive nature that could be expressed in being loving but also in outbursts of anger.

BOARDING SCHOOL

In 1929 John was sent to join his brother Philip and sister Mary at their boarding school in Seascale, sixty miles west of Skirwith. He hated it. Many tears were shed as he grieved for his lost freedom and home comforts. He was bullied and tried to get himself expelled. Meanwhile, his father accepted the position of vicar of the parish of Tilney All Saints in Norfolk. John was disappointed to discover that the flat landscape around his new family home was entirely

different from the mountainous backdrop of his earliest years, a nearby colony of grey herons providing a rare focus for his interest. Aged nine-years-old, he was moved to the King's School, Ely, but also seems to have been unhappy there, finally running away in spring 1933, walking twenty five miles back to Tilney.

John was not the only Bradburne that was unhappy with his lot: the same year that he made his escape from the King's School, his family moved to Cawston, forty miles east of Tilney. Cawston's fields and woodlands were dominated by the 150-foot spire of its Gothic church and the ample vicarage with its garden was most attractive to John. By now he had been sent to a new school – Up Pantiles – with the hope that he would learn enough to gain a scholarship to a public school. He was happier there but his father's hopes were dashed by his dreamy son's lack of aptitude. Fortunately for Reverend Bradburne a generous family friend offered to pay John's school fees and so, at the age of thirteen, he was sent as a boarder to Gresham's School in nearby Holt.

At Gresham's, John lived at Farfield House, a boarding house that had nurtured luminaries such as the composer Benjamin Britten and the poet W. H. Auden. Although he never had any notable academic success at the school, John made friends, fell in love with English literature, tried learning to play the bugle, clarinet and recorder and developed a gift for mimicry, though contemporaries recalled that this gift was never used maliciously. He was also remembered for compulsively climbing trees, the taller the better.

Despite his father's religious calling, John was not noticeably devout or even particularly interested in religion at school. Every day ended with prayers led by the boarding house prefects and there were morning and evening prayers on Sundays. Christianity was taught as an academic subject but the emphasis was less on faith but rather on personal moral conduct. For some years John enlisted in Gresham's Officers Training Corps, the prospect of camping probably acting as a particular incentive to him joining up. But perhaps more attracted him as, on leaving Gresham's at the age of eighteen, he took the entrance exam for the Royal Military College at Sandhurst. He passed the exam. It was June 1939 – the world was on the brink of war.

CHAPTER 2

War: A Gurkha in India and Malaya, a Chindit in Burma

With Britain's declaration of war against Hitler's Germany on 3rd September 1939, conscription was announced. On 24th June 1940 Bradburne was called up to attend an Officer Cadet Training Unit on Salisbury Plain. He began in August and on 20th December he was commissioned as a second lieutenant. His brother was also commissioned at this time and both requested to be posted to the Indian Army, setting out for Liverpool where they hoped to disembark. It was to be February 1941 when they finally boarded SS Mulberra, part of a convoy of vessels heading for Bombay, arriving on 15th April. There the two brothers, who had shared a cabin throughout the voyage, parted – John joining the 28th infantry in the 2nd battalion of the 9th Gurkha regiment. "The East is interesting," he thought, "even if it isn't alluring." He settled into army camp life, though retaining his love for climbing up trees and spending hours aloft playing his recorder. The Gurkhas must have been bemused by the unusual recreation of their new officer.

As it turned out, Bradburne was soon dispatched to Malaya, arriving at Port Sweetenham on 3rd September and immediately setting out for Taiping, 125 miles to the north of Port Sweetenham. It was: "one of God's own countries with one of the Devil's own climates", wrote Bradburne, "We are surrounded by high hills, covered in equatorial forest. Colours are really vivid… All in all, I like it very much, ten times as much as India."

Before embarking for Malaya, Bradburne had been trained in the use of artillery. Now he and his company trained according to the terrain of Malaya: dense vegetation, a menagerie of animals such as he had only ever read about, and suffocating heat. Meanwhile, the Japanese army was also preparing its offensive. On 8th December the 28th Japanese division landed on Malayan soil and routed British forces, destroying nearly all the aircraft and sinking a Royal Navy battleship and a battlecruiser. At first John's company was held in reserve but on 22nd December his company was called forward to assist in destroying a railway bridge and occupy a crossroads at Blanja. This was to be a rare victory as the Japanese advanced amidst carnage in the Battle of Slim

River. Hundreds of the British forces were killed or wounded and over a thousand soldiers were taken by the Japanese as prisoners. Later, Churchill was to refer to the battle as, "the worst disaster and largest capitulation in British history."

SOMETHING BEYOND US

Bradburne's company was forced into retreat. Heading for a railway bridge they found it occupied by Japanese troops. Using chunks of fallen tree trunks as buoys, most of John's troops made it to the other side of the river. His commander, Captain Hart, split the company into small groups to make their way through the jungle, then he and Bradburne set out themselves. They took a different route from the rest of the troops, making their way to the coast and thus evading capture. They had no food and survived on foraged fruit and roots, supplemented by rice from families along the riverbank who risked their lives by assisting them. Bradburne succumbed to cerebral malaria, becoming delirious and very weak. Captain Hart remained with him, helping him along.

At this most vulnerable moment, Bradburne later recorded, he felt that he experienced a vision as he gazed up towards the starry heavens: "I felt for the first time that there is something beyond us," he wrote, "if only we could get in touch with it." From that moment he also believed that he was gifted with a sixth spiritual sense, an ability to apprehend something of the beyond.

Bradburne and Hart took a month to reach the sea where they rowed a boat for sixty miles to Sumatra. They were caught up in a typhoon and were lucky to have safely landed on the Malayan coast where their little vessel sank. Meeting with a group of Highlanders who were in the same desperate straits as themselves, the group forced at gunpoint the owner of another small boat to transport them to Sumatra.

As soon as they landed at Sumatra, Bradburne was taken to a hospital, but on that very day the Japanese began their attack on the Indonesian island. So serious was Bradburne's condition that he was transferred to a hospital in the city of Medan, just before that city was bombarded by Japanese shells. He lost consciousness but, as he was later to reflect in verse, the experience of the frailty and the mortal peril that he was in was a turning point in his life. He wrote:

> I know not what disease I had
> But in Sumatra I went mad
> (With sunstroke and malaria
> Maybe) – O blest hysteria!
>
> O blest delirium that told
> Me clearly that to find The God
> Was all I really wanted! Odd.
> But thus He called me to His Fold.
> (*Ut Unum Sint*, 1956, stanzas 1410-11)

The delirium brought about various religious experiences, one of which John later identified as being about the Blessed

Virgin Mary. After ten days, as the British were evacuated from Sumatra, Bradburne was able to walk again. A four-hundred-mile journey to Padang ensued, followed by a perilous sea crossing to Ceylon (now Sri Lanka) where Captain Hart and Bradburne disembarked at Colombo. From Colombo they set sail again, this time heading to Bombay. The ship that had carried them to Colombo had been sunk by the Japanese shortly after their journey.

Throughout this time Bradburne's parents had been sent a telegram informing them that their son was missing in action. A week later they received news that he was in Sumatra. Finally on 16th March 1942, Bradburne was able to send a telegram to his parents telling them that he was safe and well.

But was he? A letter that he wrote to his parents soon after seems more like a haphazard stream of consciousness. Be that as it may, Bradburne's letter was not without meaning. "I believe," he wrote, "that having touched rock bottom, my reason is now surely founded on a desire for two things: honesty and simplicity." He then mentioned the prayers of St Ignatius of Loyola and the Apostles' Creed.

PROMOTION

Being recognised as fit enough to serve once more in the military, Bradburne was promoted to the position of battalion adjutant having been sent to the Indian city of Dehradun. It was at Dehradun that he met John Thurston

Dove, a Catholic officer a year younger than him, who was to become a lifelong friend. The two met when Dove came to Bradburne's door asking if he could play some light music on Bradburne's gramophone. Instead he found himself listening to Bach's *Jesu, Joy of Man's Desiring*, and listening to Bradburne's commentary on the music. Having got to know each other, they decided to share a military bungalow in the small town of Birpur with one another.

Life in Birpur was totally different from the traumas that Bradburne had just experienced. The officers were served by local staff and seem to have had ample free time – all in all a comfortable existence. Bradburne enjoyed the natural beauty of the region and his frequent conversations with Dove about religious themes. Briefly, he became entranced by the religions of India but it was his intuitive and emotional response to music, not least the sacred music of J. S. Bach, that he recognised as the catalyst for his emerging faith. Then, on 23rd May 1943, he wrote to his parents, "My life is dedicated to Christ once and for all."

What shape this new dedication was going to take remained, however, unclear. There were more discussions about religious questions with John Dove and Bradburne began to read about the Catholic faith. The two friends were parted in autumn 1943, Dove being deployed to the European front and Bradburne being sent to the Chindits' training camp in West Bengal. On Thursday 5th March 1944, after months of rigorous training, Bradburne boarded a

Waco CG-4 glider that was pulled by a Dakota C-47 through the skies over enemy territory to establish a stronghold they called Broadway. Approaching the planned landing site, the Waco was released to glide silently down to land. But by the time Bradburne's glider landed there were scenes of carnage on the ground: wreckage of aircraft that had crash landed or hit obstacles whilst making their descent became yet more debris for other aeroplanes to crash into. Bradburne was lucky: thirty two men died in the operation and over two hundred were wounded – that was more than half the number of men who had been dispatched for the operation.

But the endeavour was not a failure as over thirty tons of equipment had been successfully flown in and, almost miraculously, American soldiers arrived on the scene with two bulldozers which were set to work to level out the short runway. While most of the soldiers were engaged in this work others were deputed to burn the wreckage of the crashed gliders along with the bodies of the dead. With a workable runway, twelve American planes flew in, the wounded flown out and plans put in place for the first attack from behind enemy lines – blowing up a railway line. Within a week of the first perilous flights, nine thousand men had been stationed along with Bradburne.

The encampment was soon bombed by a squadron of Japanese planes and then attacked from the ground, but the English forces were able to prevail in both cases. A further attack ensued necessitating hand to hand combat but the Japanese were repelled. There were further attacks on Broadway and on a second camp set up at 'White City', twenty five miles south-west of Broadway. There were over seven hundred Japanese fatalities while one hundred Chindits were killed.

Bradburne's brigade were then moved north to the stronghold of 'Blackpool', enduring an exhausting march, sometimes on paths, at other times through the dense undergrowth. As they arrived, they were swept up almost immediately in yet another battle but this time the Japanese gained the upper hand, continually replacing their dead soldiers with fresh combatants while the British forces were running out of ammunition. Finally on 26th May 1944 the Chindits and Gurkhas began to evacuate Blackpool, making a three-day march to Mokso Sakan.

Armed with new ammunition Bradburne's company continued to battle on to Mogaung, on to Sahmaw Chaung, the platoon shelling the Japanese and suffering frequent and sustained fire themselves. By the beginning of August 1944, the Chindits and the Gurkhas had suffered many fatalities due to disease as well as enemy fire. Bradburne was among those evacuated to Bengal, then being transported by train to Dehradun. After some months of recuperation he was deployed to Burma. By 27th March 1945 he had once more been evacuated back to Dehradun due to his poor health and in June he was on his way back to England. By October he was home.

CHAPTER 3

Searching for God – England 1945-1950

By the time that Bradburne arrived home both his brother and sister had married, his father had retired and was in poor health, and the family were about to move from Norfolk to Devon. He spent ten days with his family before reporting to the military hospital in Dumfries for a medical check-up. All was well, though he was certainly emaciated, and Bradburne travelled down to Devon, renting a room in Sidbury. He did not look for a job but rather lived off his army gratuity and the proceeds from doing odd jobs around town. He seems to have spent most of his time enjoying the natural beauty of the landscape around Sidbury and the company of his new girlfriend, Anne Hardwicke. Despite his profession of faith while in the Far East, he was uncommitted to any particular religious path though still remaining deeply interested in religious questions. He attempted to read his way into faith but just became more confused as he read various books professing contrary opinions.

One morning Bradburne sought out the Catholic church in Ottery, a small chapel formed out of an old coach house. There he stumbled upon Mass being celebrated. The priest was Irish and the small congregation consisted of a little group of Marist sisters and a handful of lay people. The sisters noticed their new visitor, as did the priest, Fr Patrick Dunne, who, while preaching, held up the unknown man kneeling throughout the whole of the Mass as an example of piety. An embarrassed Bradburne fled the church, but he was back very soon; the sisters had repeatedly invited him for coffee and a chat with Fr Dunne.

Bradburne became increasingly unclear as to the way ahead in terms of religion, work and personal commitment. He records that the 'cobwebs of war' were entangled in his head. He found a job with the Forestry Commission hewing wood in the Quantock Hills and proposed to Anne Hardwicke. He was not a good woodsman but was still popular with his workmates, one of whom was a Catholic. That man, Jack Dunn, would have been very relieved when John Dove, Bradburne's Catholic friend from the army, was demobbed and went home to his parents' house just ten miles from where Bradburne was working. Bradburne had been quizzing Dunn about his faith but, as Dunn was a cradle Catholic who had never really questioned the tenets of his belief, he found his friend's questions impossible to answer. Dove and Bradburne again spent many hours discussing the Catholic faith, Bradburne considering converting to Catholicism and Dove wondering whether or not he himself was being called to the religious life. Bradburne approached Canon Richard Iles, the parish priest at Taunton, for formal instruction in the Catholic faith. He visited Buckfast Abbey, Devon, which he loved.

His father, now becoming desperate that his son should remain within the Anglican fold, suggested that Bradburne take a retreat at the Anglican Monastery of the Resurrection in Mirfield. John went and there he was introduced to the writings of St John Henry Newman, reading Newman's autobiographical *Apologia* soon after he left and being greatly influenced by what he read. His father made one final attempt to stop his son converting by writing to his nephew, Thomas Comber, a High Church priest in South Africa, asking him to encourage John by letter not to convert to Catholicism. His efforts were in vain – Bradburne abandoned his life as a forester, found temporary work on a building site and at Exeter Hospital then spent the summer in a rented room at Buckfastleigh. Dom Raphael Stones, a monk of the steadily rising Buckfast Abbey, who had lost an eye during World War One and served as a chaplain during the Second World war in Bengal and Burma (now Myanmar), prepared Bradburne for being received into the Catholic Church. In return for his meals, Bradburne assisted the monks with odd jobs, tending their vegetable garden and the cemetery. He still needed an income so found work as a bricklayer.

RECEIVED AND CONFIRMED

On the Feast of Christ the King, 26th October 1947 (the last Sunday in October), Bradburne was received into the Catholic Church in the Abbey's Chapel of St Anne and was confirmed two days later. Many years later, Bradburne reflected on why he had become a Catholic:

> I wanted to be sure of salvation. I came to the conclusion that there could not be more than one true Church that Christ had founded, and by the Grace of God I got there. There was in me a great desire to belong to a society which could embrace a maximum, and not an exclusive minimum of people on their way to Heaven. The influence of India and four and a half years in the East stirred my mind a good deal. I was deeply influenced by a friend of mine [John Dove] with me in the army out there.

Having begun to consider whether or not he might have a vocation to monastic life, Bradburne decided to break off his engagement to Anne Hardwicke. Despite his enthusiasm, the Abbot discerned that, as was the custom with converts, Bradburne should wait for two years before entering the monastery. Nonetheless, he was designated by the monastic community as a 'provisional postulant', but told to find a job for the time being. The monks probably recommended him as a teacher to the headmaster of a boys' preparatory school, Gaveney House, in the holiday resort of Exmouth. There he became a popular schoolmaster, not least because of his humour and kindness, teaching eight to ten-year-olds general subjects. One pupil later wrote: "Have you ever known a saint? I have, I think. For a brief period one of our teachers was John Randal Bradburne."

At about the time of his conversion to Catholicism, Bradburne's propensity for articulating his thoughts, feelings and prayers in poetic verse blossomed and flourished into an output that was so prodigious (he had written more than five thousand poems by the end of his life) that he earned himself a place in *The Guinness Book of Records* as the most prolific poet in the English language.

Whilst at Gaveney, Bradburne became friendly with a fellow teacher, Margaret Smith, and soon fell in love. Smith was sixteen years older than Bradburne, yet they shared much in common, including a love of music. As Smith became aware of the intensity of Bradburne's feelings for her she attempted to let him see that she sought friendship, not marital love. But Bradburne's passion got the better of him as, somewhat indiscreetly, during a school cricket match he declared his love for her and proposed to her. Greatly embarrassed, she first gently then with angry exasperation asked Bradburne to keep quiet in case their conversation was overheard by the pupils. Bradburne stormed away from the match and out of the school, walking and walking, never turning back, marching the twenty three miles back to Buckfast. The two never met again, Margaret Smith having no idea how her friend spent the rest of his life until the day when she heard of his death in a BBC radio report from Zimbabwe (called Rhodesia under colonial rule).

Back at Buckfast, Dom Raphael advised Bradburne to find a job but before doing so he and John Dove decided to make a pilgrimage to Lourdes. Dove later recalled how initially, Bradburne had found, "so much ceremony," in honour of the Blessed Virgin Mary to be, "rather over-bearing." Yet, having travelled to the shrine by sea and train, the two friends joined a pilgrim group led by a Benedictine who advised his hearers to "[allow the Mother of God] to show herself," to them in her own way. Dove noted that Bradburne heeded this advice and, "it later led to a close and extraordinary bond."

On their return to England Dove entered the Society of Jesus whilst Bradburne, having hitchhiked to Lancashire with a friend, briefly took up the work of stoker on a trawler. He hated it and resolved once again to seek monastic life, this time presenting himself to the Carthusians at Parkminster, Sussex. He was accepted as a lay-brother and appointed as doorkeeper. As his musical gifts were clearly apparent, he was also permitted to join the monks in singing The Offices in choir. The austerity of the Carthusian way of life greatly appealed to Bradburne, as did the solitary nature of their existence – meeting together each day only to pray and once a week for recreation together. But it was a demanding life all the same, having to rise in the early hours for Matins and Lauds, living in an unheated room and going to pray in the freezing church. His stay with the Carthusians did not last long – just over six months.

TO BE A PILGRIM

Bradburne was on his way once more in the summer of 1950, this time heading for Rome on pilgrimage and hoping to beg his way onwards to the Holy Land. Rome left him agog with wonder and he was thrilled to see Pope Pius XII on two occasions. With merely a bag full of belongings – including his shaving gear, a Roman Missal, the English Hymnal and a copy of the Psalms, Bradburne meandered down to Naples with the intention of sailing to Cyprus by way of Sicily and Greece and then on to the Holy Land. He struck up a friendship with some Franciscans en route and the friars encouraged him in his quest. Their influence and inspiration were to prove lifelong for Bradburne.

On making land at Haifa, Bradburne immediately set out for Nazareth. "How wonderful it was to be driving through the twilight, up and up, beyond the fertile plains, to Nazareth," he wrote, "where the Word was made flesh, and spent nearly thirty years in his visible life on Earth." His sense of the holiness of the ground he was treading grew and grew: "I was walking in NAZARETH, where the King of Kings so often walked, where he ran and played as a boy."

From Nazareth, Bradburne hitched lifts to Cana, Tiberius, Tel Aviv and finally to Jerusalem, arriving there in time for the third anniversary of his conversion. He had left Rome with just five British pounds yet, "Helpers of one kind and another seemed to be posted along the way, and to have got here for this Feast of the King, my third anniversary, is a joy indeed."

All along the journey Bradburne had seen himself in the guise of a missionary setting his heart on bringing the Jewish people to see Christ as the Saviour of the world. The Feast of Christ the King was of paramount importance to him, as he related in an interview in 1965: "My concern for the Jews dated chiefly from my thinking about the Gospel of that feast – 'Art thou the King of the Jews?' I thought what a pity that he is not since he was born in Judah." In over 150 poems he wrote of his dedication to Christ the King and, at the time of his conversion, spoke of how he hoped that he would be worthy of dying the death of a martyr for his king.

In Jerusalem, Bradburne was given shelter at the House of Ratisbonne, which belonged to the Community of Our Lady's Fathers of Sion, an order founded to promote understanding between Christians and Jews and to bring the Jewish people to Christ. It was, it seemed to Bradburne, providential that he had been directed to this place. For seven weeks he remained, being given board and lodging in return for sweeping and gardening, pumping water and collecting olives. Exhilarated as he was by the Holy City, Bradburne also endured darker emotions, at one point writing to John Dove: "My soul's a desert just now, and I had today a fearful go of black depression and doubt. But I am learning to recognise these attacks not as signs of failure but of victory and progress."

The superior of the community, Fr de Conde, greatly impressed Bradburne as he saw his good humour and ability to be comfortable with everyone, no matter how rich or poor. Likewise, Bradburne impressed the superior with his devoutness and zeal; Fr de Conde asked Bradburne if he might not think of joining the community. At first Bradburne was reticent about this, believing that he did not have a vocation to be a priest but Fr de Conde persuaded him otherwise and made arrangements for Bradburne to join the novitiate at Louvain.

With references from Buckfast obtained, other formalities attended to and after a few lessons in Latin and French, Bradburne left Jerusalem on 13th September 1950, sailing from Haifa to Marseilles and then travelling by train to Louvain via Paris and Brussels and finally arriving at the house of the Fathers of Sion on 22nd December. Just over a week later he wrote to John Dove:

All the odd pieces of my jig-saw are falling into place, I wonder whether I will see the full picture on earth; not that it matters – the present moment being a Sacrament full of God…one is made somewhat solitary through not knowing much French. But I love solitude – too much, I fear. And thus, I am very happy, very certain that this is where I must be and stay…I feel as if I'd come to port after a long stormy time at sea. Now my ship can be repaired and fitted well for more 'voyaging'. I speak only in a spiritual sense of course. My vagabondage is done, and I'm under orders as you are.

MUTUAL FORGIVENESS

His new state of life brought peace not only to John Bradburne but also to his father, Thomas. Thomas Bradburne had, for some years, been distressed and worried by the lack of direction that he saw in his son's life and by his conversion to the Catholic Faith. But on learning of his son's entering the novitiate at Louvain he wrote to him:

I hardly know what to say or how to thank you for your generosity in thanking me for anything which I may have been the means under God, of doing for you. And do remember that whatever stresses and strains between us there may have been in the past – as were almost inevitably bound to arise in this our present state of imperfection – there cannot now or ever be any question of mutual unforgiveness. Any shadow of that across our lives shall,

please God, be banished forever. Otherwise dear lad we could not approach our respective altars which would mean the outer darkness for one or other of us.

Bradburne's eighteen months at Louvain was, he considered, "highly profitable" and, "spiritually essential". He reflected on his life writing to a friend:

I travelled via the Carthusians to Rome and Jerusalem and Louvain, because…l believe in following my dreams …I follow the Holy Spirit to whose Church I belong. My course has been erratic and zig-zag, but that has been the fault of no one but myself […]

As to my part with [women] it has been a crazy course, of which I accuse myself of much sin and sadness, but in which I thank God for much blessedness and happiness. How he saved them from me, and me for Himself, only He knows. Certainly I am unfit for marriage (even if I'd been 'successful' as you put it). But there is a positive way of seeing it, viz. it is God's will because I am fit for something else. His love only. And He is All and in all.

CLEAR AND IRRESISTIBLE CALL

In July 1952 Bradburne once again left the possibility of a settled life believing that he had, "a clear and irresistible call of God my King to be His tramp and set my steps towards Jerusalem." His superior at Louvain seems to have recognised this giving his departing postulant a warm letter of recommendation:

John Bradburne is a convert from Protestantism who aspires to the life of a perfect Christian. Different attempts have led him to the conclusion that he is not suited to the sedentary religious life; rather he feels himself drawn to imitate the example of a Saint Benedict (Joseph) Labre or a Pere de Foucauld. It is in order to follow this way, of his own free will, that he has left our House in Louvain where he has spent a year and where he has left only happy memories.

Writing to John Dove, Bradburne declared:

Please always consider me as a monk, a monk of Our Lady and a vagabond of God. Saint Francis Bernadone (Francis of Assisi) is my spiritual master – but no imitation. Let us imitate the KING, so shall we be true originals. O pray, pray that I may follow Him well and fulfil my odd role in this short Earthly Play and sojourn.

Bradburne set out once again for the Holy Land, hitchhiking his way across France to Italy, foraging and begging for food, sleeping in the fields and such shelters as he could find. He found his way to the mountain town of Palma in Italy's Campania region. There the parish priest, Don Francesco Picchiocchi, let him sleep in the organ loft of the parish church in return for Bradburne acting as sacristan. The setting seemed ideal: living and working in a sacred building, having an organ on which to play and the instrument's bench to use as a table on which he could write his poems.

The townsfolk must have been somewhat bemused by their eccentric English guest and surprised at his willingness to help about the place, even offering to collect the rubbish, a kindness that eventually won him the official paid role of assistant dustman.

Bradburne kept in correspondence with his father throughout his travels and, at Christmas 1952, he received from him what was to turn out to be his father's last letter, a letter that John Bradburne was to keep for the rest of his life. His father wrote:

It was a great joy for me to get your letter today and to know of your happiness and welfare with your feet safely set upon the way which in my old age I am coming to see more and more clearly is God's way for you, dear boy. Thank you so very much. So in any of your thoughts of me or of yourself in relationship to me as your father, you must never think or feel that there is any need either to explain, still less to apologise [...]

I like to think of you in your organ loft. But I do hope you get your proper and sufficient share of sleep and rest – for we are not out of Brother Ass the body yet.

As a further token of fatherly care for his son, Thomas Bradburne added a postscript to the letter promising his son that, "As a link between us henceforth I will say the Creed, the Lord's Prayer and the Hail Mary in the holy tongue [Latin]." Five months later Thomas Bradburne was dead and with his death, John Bradburne's time in Palma came to an end as, of all his siblings, he was the one most available to care for his elderly mother back in Devon. Once she had sent him enough money to make the journey home, he set out arriving in September 1953.

A few months before his father's death, in the parish church of Palma, Bradburne had an intense spiritual experience that drew him to dedicate himself to the Blessed Virgin Mary, a dedication that grew steadily until his death. It was 2nd February 1953 (the Feast of Candlemas). He later recorded his experience in verse:

> Drawn by my Belle I'll call myself her bow
> And not without a touch of vanity; At Candlemas,
> at half-past-six or so,
> I married her in Nineteen Fifty Three.

RETURN TO ENGLAND

His time at home with his mother was only to last a few weeks. The solitary life which he had grown used to as he journeyed abroad as well as his time in Palma had increased his sense that part of his vocation was to live a life apart from others.

Through friends he found a garden hut nearby in Ottery St Mary that he used as a hermitage, remaining there for a year living on brown bread, apples and cider. There he prayed following the monastic hours and there he wrote and wrote poems. When he ventured out he might have been found on street corners playing his recorder, doing his bit to raise funds for the restoration of the local church. A journalist reported in a local paper:

> The young man, with his closely-cropped hair and cultured accent, talks with the evangelistic zeal of an early apostle, lives a frugal life […] and calls himself, "the Jester of Christ the King". From the wooden recorder, expertly played, dangled dozens of coloured ribbons […] I listened as old English airs floated out over the Cathedral Close and then asked him what the coloured ribbons were in aid of. He gave me a friendly smile, and replied, "Just to give the air of gaiety an Elizabethan jester ought to have; for we are Elizabethans, you know!" He told me he was a poet whom nobody had yet recognised. ("They probably will do in another 60 years.") "Don't you have any permanent sort of occupation?" I asked. His eyes twinkled as he replied, "Nothing is permanent in this life."

From the garden hut, Bradburne moved to an old house belonging to the nuns of Ottery St Mary. From there he moved to a friend's garden cottage and from there, in the spring of 1955, he moved to London, returning briefly to Buckfast before going back to London once more.

He survived as a street musician for some months before John Dove suggested that he once again tested his vocation, this time at the Benedictine Prinknash Abbey in

Gloucestershire. He entered the monastery as a postulant in November 1955, thought himself happy beyond anything he had ever known and yet four months later, on the evening of Good Friday 1956, he slipped away quietly from the abbey, leaving behind, for the last time, any attempt to enter a religious congregation.

From Prinknash, Bradburne returned to Ottery St Mary, finding work on a farm and living in a loft above the stables. For his prayer life he took the obligations of a Franciscan Tertiary as his model, saying or singing the Little Office of the Blessed Virgin Mary as a liturgical devotion, the day and night marked out by the rhythm of its prayers. As ever, he did not stay long, returning to London towards the end of 1956 to live on the streets playing his recorder, until he found a job as a domestic at St Mary Abbot's Hospital. He found solace in Westminster Cathedral, in particular enjoying the singing of its renowned choir.

WESTMINSTER AND BEYOND

In late October 1956, Bradburne asked for a job in the Burns & Oates bookshop across the road from Westminster Cathedral. With Christmas approaching, the shop's manager was looking for extra hands for the seasonal surge in business and gladly took Bradburne on. He offered his services to the cathedral choir too, which were politely declined, but, in the New Year, he was more successful in obtaining the position of fifth sacristan at the cathedral. While the work was congenial to him he was less than perfect in ensuring that cruets, books and vestments were always in the right place at the right time.

All the same, the chief sacristan of the time spoke of Bradburne as, "One of the most lovable men I ever knew […] a most conscientious worker." In the cathedral the newly appointed archbishop, William Godfrey, also seems to have noticed John and would spend time with him amiably chatting as the sacristan went about his duties and the archbishop paused between his long periods of prayer.

In his spare time Bradburne still wandered the streets playing his recorder. If he was given any money by passersby, he would give it to beggars or put it in the St Vincent de Paul collection box. On one occasion he was seen by a cathedral parishioner playing his recorder outside St Paul's Cathedral. The parishioner mentioned this to Westminster Cathedral's administrator, who quickly took Bradburne to task for bringing Westminster's reputation into disrepute by begging outside the Anglican cathedral. Bradburne explained that he wasn't begging but simply playing Marian hymns and giving any proceeds to the poor.

By the summer of 1957, Archbishop Godfrey invited Bradburne to become the caretaker of his country house at Hare Street, Buntingford, a Hertfordshire village some forty miles from London. This residence had been left to the Archbishops of Westminster by the Benson family, having been owned by Robert Hugh Benson, a renowned convert, priest and writer who was also the son of an Archbishop of Canterbury. The setting must, at first, have seemed ideal to Bradburne. Whilst working at Westminster Cathedral he had lived in either miniscule lodgings or shared rooms in a small flat. Hare Street House and its garden gave John much space, not least because, for the most part, he was the solitary resident, the archbishop and his staff usually being resident in Westminster.

"It is heaven to be alone with God," he wrote, "Heaven albeit with a heavy cross – that of being alone all with oneself." He continued to live as frugally as he always had, the account set up in his name revealing an unrelieved diet of baked beans, bread and margarine, and his writing of poetry burgeoned.

When Archbishop Godfrey was staying at Hare Street House, John would often serve his Mass and seek him out for conversation, seeing the archbishop as a holy man, "always up the mountain with God." When the archbishop was not in residence, Bradburne would make his way to Buntingford, two miles away, for the early morning Mass before returning to work for the morning. He would sometimes lock himself away for a week at a time for prayer and meditation. At other times he would practice on the harmonium in the house's chapel, wherein Robert Hugh Benson was buried, or spend time reading Benson's novels.

Bradburne became so immersed in the novels of Benson and felt himself so imbued by his spirit that he became very protective of Hare Street House as it had been left by Benson: alterations were not welcomed. This quickly led to altercations between Bradburne and the architect for the archbishop's secretary, Monsignor Derek Worlock (the future Archbishop of Liverpool). With Archbishop Godfrey being created a cardinal and approving a wholesale restoration of the house, Monsignor Worlock came to inspect ongoing work up to three times a month, increasing tensions between the two men whose characters were so vastly different. Yet the monsignor did much to make sure that Bradburne was as comfortable as possible in his role as caretaker.

On the whole, when they met, Bradburne was civil to Worlock, but in letters he could be blisteringly brusque. Ultimately he could bear what he saw as the destruction of Hare Street House no longer and, on 21st October 1961, he took his leave of his employment, quietly leaving Hare Street just after Cardinal Godfrey had arrived, being sure that the Blessed Sacrament in the Chapel was not left unguarded.

EVER ONWARDS

Where to from Hertfordshire? What to do next? There was, of course, no plan. With just his Gladstone bag and his recorder and, praying to St Francis of Assisi for inspiration, he stayed briefly with friends before returning to a friend's house in Devon. He decided to visit Skirwith, the home of his early years, and was immensely moved by his father's successor as vicar there, inviting him to stay the night in the house of his birth.

Returning to Devon, Bradburne briefly entertained the hope of living as a poet, writing to one friend:

If ever you look at the verses and edit them, comb them remorselessly: let nothing but gold go forth for glory. The first £300 are for you! Or if it is only 3/- have a drink, or if it is nothing (which is more likely) drink to our further success.

Having attempted to live as a hermit in a cave on the edge of Dartmoor, a friend was able to offer him the use of a small cottage in Talaton, Devon, until it was sold. Then he moved on to Cobham in Surrey, staying with his brother Philip's first wife, Esmé, helping out in the garden in return for board and lodging. She remembered him as, "a lot of fun," but also, "quite infuriating at times":

One respected his intense religious feeling, but his dogmatic insistence that the Bible was literally true in every detail and his assertion that the Catholic Church was always right led to frantic arguments for a while – until we realised that it was no good, and reverted to more mundane things.

From there Bradburne wrote to Fr John Dove, asking him if he knew of any caves in Africa where he might be able to live a solitary existence. Fr Dove, then secretary to the Archbishop of Salisbury (Harare), wrote back offering a slightly different mode of existence in Southern Rhodesia – that of a volunteer working in the Catholic Mission. For someone almost intrinsically incapable of dealing with bureaucracy John persevered in filling in the forms and undergoing medical tests and producing references so that, finally on 6th August 1962, the Feast of the Transfiguration of the Lord, John Bradburne set off for the Franciscan Mission of St Mary at Wedza in Southern Rhodesia.

CHAPTER 4

Zimbabwe

Southern Rhodesia, as it was at the time of Bradburne's arrival in August 1962, had effectively been part of the British Empire for more than seventy years. At the end of the following year the country left the Central African Federation, a colonial group of three South African territories. By this time the Rhodesian Front, a conservative and white political party dedicated to keeping Southern Rhodesia as part of the Empire, had been in power for a year and was to remain in power until the country's independence in 1979. It officially become Zimbabwe in 1980. African nationalist organisations had been banned since 1959 but were increasingly activating resistance fighters leading to guerrilla warfare from 1973. Bradburne arrived in a country of increasing racial tension between the black and the white population.

Bradburne was greeted at the airport by John Dove who was, as archbishop's secretary, also greeting the arrival of the Archbishop of Milan, the future Pope St Paul VI, on the same day. At first Dove took Bradburne to the Jesuit Mission of Chishawasha, thirteen miles west of Salisbury (now Zimbabwe's capital city Harare), then, with the archbishop, he visited the Monte Cassino Mission seventy miles east of the capital. After a visit to the Franciscans at Waterfalls, Dove and Bradburne drove one hundred miles south-east of Salisbury to the mission at Wedza, a mission that covered an area about a quarter of the size of Ireland.

Whatever assistance the Irish Franciscans had been hoping to receive from Bradburne, they soon discovered that it would not be forthcoming. He was immensely impractical, could not drive and showed little interest in learning the local language, Shona. He was likeable and clearly was fascinated by the diversity of the natural world in which he had been immersed but was unsettled by the hustle and bustle of the busy missionary station.

Two months after having arrived at Wedza, Bradburne was moved to the Franciscan mission at Enkeldoorn (now Chivhu), eighty five miles south of Harare. There he joined Fr Seán Gildea and obtained a driving licence. He had a series of minor accidents while driving so it was thought better for him to take to the wheel only in necessity. However, Bradburne and Gildea became good friends, Bradburne remaining at Enkeldoorn until mid-1963 when Gildea was moved to another mission station. At this time Bradburne was himself relocated to the newly established mission station of St Anthony's at Gandachibvuva. The superior of this mission was Fr Pascal Slevin and Bradburne moved in with him. Bradburne and the assistant priest did not get on so it was decided that Bradburne should move out of the house and, Slevin seeing that Bradburne needed solitude in order to pray, suggested that he set up a hermitage in a little brick shed on top of a nearby hill.

Had Bradburne at last found a place where he could settle? It certainly seemed so. He found a piece of asbestos roofing and set it on bricks to make a bed, covering it with a blanket. A chest and box served as a table and chair. When not praying or writing poetry he gathered firewood for the mission and helped administer medicine in the mission clinic. The mission chickens became his care too – he gave them names, the two cockerels being 'Earl of Ganda' and 'Duke of Chibvuva'. "The place beggars description," he wrote to his mother, so enamoured was he by his surroundings.

Desiring to assimilate as much of local life as possible, Bradburne learned to make the staple foods *sadza* and *muriwo*, *sadza* being a thick porridge or polenta-like dough made from maize meal, and *muriwo* being vegetables like cabbage, spring greens, spinach and kale. Thus nourished, he set about writing poetry with fresh vigour and once again hoped that his verse would be published. The failure to achieve publication was a bitter disappointment for Bradburne. Writing to his mother, he declared:

> I am reconciled now to my verse being quite unrecognised whilst I am on earth. But as I have already said, through it the name of Bradburne will ring down future centuries and that for the good. Meanwhile my life is totally obscure, but through God's grace I am happy and well, and will continue to write verses, verses that rhyme and have music in their words. Untortured, untwisted, unmodish verses [...]
>
> I do not really hate the human race, but have only verses to offer it and it has been hitherto highly scornful and treated me with the lowest contempt. To blazes with it until it comes to its senses in Heaven! I continue to write, confident never to see my work published in this life. Never mind. Posterity and Immortality are the things.

HEAVEN'S MERCY

How does a reader interpret such an emotional outpouring? Bradburne's confidence in his own poetic abilities was somewhat childlike. His poetry certainly gives insights into his self-understanding: "This life of mine will have been such an utter failure," he opined, "if nothing comes of this talent God has given me, setting aside the matter of personal salvation, which Heaven's mercy may arrange. An artist's joy consists in seeing his joy passed on and communicated to many people. Otherwise production becomes mere frustration. According to the superior of the Ganda mission:

John was a tower of strength at Gandachibvuva. What else could a man of prayer be? The new Mission was blessed with his presence. He refused to stay with us at the Mission and took up residence on the hill, making the little shed which supported the water tank his residence. This accommodation he gladly shared with the hens.

Once a week John joined us down at the Mission house for a meal. His own cooking of sadza and vegetable supplied his modest requirements of food for the rest of the time. What an example in Poverty. What a joy emanated from his person. John was close to His Lord.

Three times a day John rang a bell, calling the Mission and the surrounding area to prayer. At six, twelve and six his voice was raised in praise of Him who gave us Mary as our Mother. Frequently, apart from these times, the strains of John's voice could be heard raised to the Father in prayer. How secure we felt in the knowledge that 'the hermit' entertained Love itself on the hill. Our work must be blessed.

Each morning John prepared the altar for the celebration of the Holy Sacrifice and he served. Frequently during the day John could be seen in the presence of the Blessed Sacrament. There he used to sing God's praises.

I vividly remember erecting the Stations of the Cross in the Church with John present. We would have to have something special. John agreed and suggested we sing the 'Stabat Mater' which we did. I remember him saying it was a privilege for him to be at such a ceremony. In later days I frequently saw him walking the Way of the Cross.

Bradburne's 'example of poverty' was greatly admired. Stories, such as when he gave an old woman his only blanket after all her belongings had been destroyed in a hut fire, and how he gave away his shoes, walking barefoot for months, were remembered long after he left Ganda.

CHANGE AND CHANGE

At the beginning of 1964 it was decided that the mission where Bradburne lived had to expand, necessitating demolition of the shed in which he lived. He was asked to leave but the contract that both he and the Franciscans had signed before he travelled to Africa guaranteed that the order would pay his airfare to whatever part of the world that he chose when he was no longer to be engaged in working for the Franciscans.

After some thought, Bradburne decided to go to a Tibetan monastery. This plan fell through so instead he decamped to M'bebi farm in the Mazoe Valley (Mazowe), thirty miles north of Harare. No wonder he wrote to his mother that, "Life becomes for me more and more of a definable pattern of change and change, and I am in no way daunted by the apparent failure of it and waste of education it may seem."

At M'bebi, Bradburne acted as caretaker of a property that had recently been given to the Jesuits, living there alone with a cat until the Jesuits took up residence. The solitary life remained almost essential to Bradburne, giving him the space to pray and to write. It was also in 1964 that a television producer in Harare, having heard of Bradburne's gifts of wit and mimicry combined in an engaging personality, invited him to audition as a television presenter. He passed and, for eight months, chaired discussion programmes, a role that he found stressful and was glad to give up.

In December 1964, the Jesuit novitiate moved to M'bebi and Bradburne went to live with John Dove at Silveira House Jesuit centre, on the outskirts of Harare. Despite living in a community house, Bradburne was able to carve out space for himself. He continued his practice of singing The Office and repaid his keep by acting as a caretaker for the premises. With the arrival of a harmonium in the chapel, he was able to gather a small choir together with whom he taught to sing Bach and from whom he learnt how to sing Shona hymns.

SOLITARY SAMARITAN

A further interest of Bradburne's during his time living near Harare was volunteering as a Samaritan in the city. It was while assisting a suicidal man in 1966 that Bradburne met a lady called Joan to whom he became close, relating to her, as he had done to no other, his traumatic experiences of the Second World War and his own feelings of fear and anger caused by them.

It would be unsurprising if some of the stranger aspects of Bradburne's behaviour were not the result of undiagnosed post-traumatic distress that had exacerbated his consistently natural yet somewhat quirky behaviour. An example of his unusual character is that, seeking solitude, Bradburne actively encouraged a swarm of bees to take up residence in a hive under his desk. He loved the bees but was also more than aware that others were happy not to enter his room as he typed his poetry with the bees flying freely around him.

By 1966, Dove and Bradburne had been joined at Silveira House by some very able and willing missionary helpers. The presence of more people, let alone their ability to manage car repairs and other practical jobs, made Bradburne doubt his own usefulness and yearn to be more alone once more. He moved out of Silveira House into a shack by its hen house until Dove coaxed him back inside again by giving him a small room that was set apart from the more active parts of the building.

Bees were not the only wildlife that Bradburne enjoyed – for a time he had the pleasure of the company of a tame bateleur eagle that a friend had given him for safekeeping. The bird was Bradburne's prize and joy until, having gone missing, it was found dead near the Jesuit house.

That tensions were rising within Southern Rhodesia must have been clear to Bradburne, especially after its government's unilateral declaration of independence from the United Kingdom on 11 November 1965. However it was only in 1967, in a letter to his mother, that he first wrote of the situation. Bradburne was scathing about the government – which he described as an "unenlightened petty state" and a "Puppet State" – and its intentions to legislate for apartheid. Apartheid was already a reality in Rhodesia and was especially noticeable in the many townships around Salisbury. He wrote, "I think an insistence on the nature of the Incarnate God with His decidedly coloured skin would be a timely and sublime objection."

In April 1968, Dove and Bradburne returned to England together for a holiday. Having spent three weeks with his mother, Bradburne went on to visit other friends including the monks at Buckfast in Devon. Dove and Bradburne took their leave of each other in London as Bradburne had decided to return to the Holy Land once more to be a missioner of Christ. From England to Belgium; by train on to Venice and by sea from Venice on to Haifa; from there by bus on to Jerusalem. Bradburne made his way to the Wailing Wall where, over five days, he sang the Lamentations of Jeremiah to music by François Couperin, a French Baroque composer. He also recited, on three occasions, the Little Office of the Blessed Virgin Mary after which he looked for, but could not find, work to earn some money.

Realising that he could not stay, Bradburne travelled via Malta to Libya where his brother, Philip, was working for Mobil Oil. For the second leg of the journey he could only afford to take a cattle boat, which reached Tripoli at the end of June 1968.

In Tripoli, Bradburne lodged with his brother and, at first, enjoyed the social gatherings that Philip hosted at his home. But very soon Bradburne's besetting issue of irascibility, a characteristic that seems to have been present from childhood onwards, got the better of him. It was not long before he was once again attempting to make plans to return to the Holy Land – plans that included the idea of throwing away his passport in order to attempt to enter Israel unnoticed and, he thought, be somehow in a better position to find employment.

Ultimately, after sharing his hopes in letters to his mother and John Dove, he was persuaded that the best course of action was for him to return to Harare, Dove booking a flight for him from Rome. Taking leave of his brother, Bradburne would not have known that they would never meet again. Nor could he have known that he was about to discover his true vocation in life.

MTEMWA

Having returned to his little room at Silveira House and to his routine of singing *The Divine Office*, Bradburne once again set out to help the running of the mission in such ways as he was able. In March 1969 a good friend of his, Heather Benoy, invited Bradburne to join her as she set out to investigate a leper camp eighty seven miles north-east of Harare. Benoy had heard accounts of atrocious conditions at the camp and wanted to discover whether the reports were true. The camp was called Mtemwa, a Shona place name that could be translated as 'you are cut off'.

Mtemwa, forty years earlier, had been home to over two thousand lepers but, by the late 1960s, medical advances had allowed most lepers to return to their homes. In 1959 those in the community at Mtemwa who had been cured of leprosy but had remained in the camp were ordered to leave. Despite this, some two hundred remained in the camp, mainly those who had been left severely deformed by the disease. These victims either refused to leave to face discrimination and mockery in their home villages or simply were unable to leave. By 1969 the ravages of neglect and abuse by those in charge had reduced the camp of some eighty or so souls to lives of squalor and misery.

Benoy and Bradburne arrived at Mtemwa driving through an avenue of mature jacaranda trees. Their first sight was of a modest house and, beyond that in the verdant greenery of the rainy season, they could see the lepers' huts. As they walked towards these huts the horror of what they had heard of the place became real: hideously deformed men and women, their faces and limbs contorted by their shared dreadful disease, their fingernails dislocated, their bodies filthy and covered with untreated sores. On seeing the unexpected visitors, the lepers retreated to their huts only to re-emerge with sacks or blankets over their heads. As one crawled through the mud on all fours, Bradburne could only utter, in total disbelief at the hell that he was witnessing, "My God! My God!" Disbelief turned to anger as he learnt that the lepers had been ordered, by the director of the centre, to cover their faces if any visitors came to the camp, and as he saw an elderly lady covered in mud and licking a bowl on the ground.

EMOTIONAL TURMOIL

Disgusted and intending to report what she had seen, Benoy was desperate to leave the camp and return to Harare to report the conditions to the authorities. Bradburne, however, resorted to his tried and tested way of discerning the will of God: he prayed, tossed a coin in the air to decide what to do next, and declared that he was going to stay. Benoy could not believe what she was now hearing and begged Bradburne to at least return with her to explain the situation to Fr Dove and collect his belongings. Finally, Bradburne acquiesced, and agreed to return. Bradburne was in emotional turmoil. Back in Harare he talked through his conundrum with John Dove who later recalled his friend's words at the time:

> You know, I don't think that I could be very useful at Mtemwa because I've never been a boy-scout. I don't know anything about medicine, and they are in a very, very poor and serious state. They are dying of neglect. They have been treated appallingly. At any rate, I'm a reject, they are rejects, so I think we will understand each other... And so I go down on that ticket.

Almost immediately upon arriving back in Harare Bradburne distilled into verse his feelings:

> In that I've always loved to be alone
> I've treated human beings much as lepers,
> For this poetic justice may atone
> My way with God's, whose ways are always helpers;

> I did not ever dream that I might go
> And dwell amidst a flock of eighty such
> Nor did I scheme towards it ever,
> The prospect looms not to my liking much [...]

Bradburne prayed for strength to follow what he was convinced was a calling from God for him to care for the lepers of Mtemwa. Meanwhile John Dove made inquiries into who was responsible for the camp. He discovered that in 1966, a retired farmer from Harare, Philip Dighton, had visited Mtemwa and was also appalled by what he discovered. Dighton made contact with the Jesuits and, together with a Jesuit priest, Edward Ennis, an agreement was drawn up with the Department of Labour and Social Welfare, the government department that had oversight of the camp, so that the Archdiocese of Salisbury could, backed by government finances, restore the camp. A committee was set up to fundraise for any expenses that were incurred that went beyond the agreement with the department.

Dove discovered that the Jesuits had been trying, but had failed, to find a new caretaker for the camp. Dighton and Bradburne met after which Bradburne was appointed Camp Superintendent of Mtemwa and given a small salary. Among his duties Bradburne was in charge of bookkeeping, responsible for the camp's orderlies and other administrative duties – aspects of the job that he knew that he would hate and believed himself hopelessly incompetent at fulfilling.

Yet if this was the personal cost, Bradburne was more than ready to pay the price.

At first Bradburne was adamant that he would live in one of the leper huts and even went as far in his desire to identify as closely with those for whom he was to care as expressing his hope that he too might catch leprosy. When informed that if he did succumb to the disease he would be moved to a European leprosarium, he finally agreed to lodging in a refitted butcher's shop on the edge of the camp. On 1st August 1969 John Bradburne moved to Mtemwa – he was to remain there until his death.

Upon arriving at his new home, Bradburne set about learning the names of the seventy eight lepers at the camp and introduced himself to Dr Luisa Guidotti and the religious sisters who were stationed at the All Souls Mission eleven miles north of Mtemwa and were responsible for the medical needs of the camp. Two weeks after arriving at the camp, Bradburne wrote frankly to his mother about the stresses and strains of his new life, admitting to having just downed a triple brandy after a particularly trying day but asking her to pray hard, "that drink NOT my consolation be."

CHAPTER 5

Daily Life in the Leper Camp

Each of Bradburne's days at Mtemwa were structured by his singing of The Office and his daily recitation of the Rosary. At the heart of his main room he constructed, from boxes, cartons and tins, what he referred to as his 'Ark of the Covenant'. The ark was built in the shape of a pyramid and was covered in rosaries, crosses, shells, cards, ribbons, ornaments and pieces of paper on which Bradburne had written his poems. It was ever changing in its appearance as Bradburne added or subtracted various elements of its decoration. One element of this focal point of Bradburne's devotion was the Bible that he reverently kept at the bottom of the pyramid. For Bradburne, calling the shrine the 'Ark of the Covenant' reminded him of the ark that was the most treasured possession of the people of Israel and contained the stone tablets on which the Ten Commandments had 'been' written. 'Ark' also reminded him of the Blessed Virgin Mary, one of whose titles is 'Ark of the Covenant' in reference to carrying the child Jesus, the very word of God incarnate, in her womb. To prayer, Bradburne added mortification, eating and sleeping as little as he possibly could and referring to his physical body as Brother Ass.

A priest that was based near Mtemwa and who became a close friend of Bradburne, Fr David Gibbs, recorded that a typical day for Bradburne would start at dusk with the chanting of The Office in his hut. Throughout the night, if not attending to a dying or very sick leper, he would pray and meditate and, "when the Muse came", write poetry. Early in the morning he would run a mile, "just to keep fit," before washing and going to open the chapel. A morning service would follow where prayers were offered, the scriptures heard and Holy Communion distributed, Bradburne also playing the organ for the service. Then, Fr Gibbs writes:

The voices die away, the organ stops, the doors of the church are opened and the lepers file out led by 'Baba' [father] John carrying a basket. As the lepers come out of the chapel, having just received the Body of Christ, they stop to chat to Baba John. Some just say 'hello', others ask for medicine for a headache, a cough, a cold, malaria, itching body or sore eyes. 'Baba' delves into his basket and produces a bottle, a tube, a few capsules, an ointment, a cream or just a few sweets for those who need cheering up.

There is something for everybody. Spiritually fulfilled, materially helped, the lepers move off to their huts happy, cared for and at peace with God and with each other. Some walk, others crawl and still others are wheeled away in wheelchairs.

SERVING THE SICK

After a light breakfast, Bradburne would visit every leper every day. He brought food to them and dressed their wounds; he washed those of them that were unable to do this themselves and cleaned the ground between their huts of rubbish; he carried those who could not otherwise move, gathered firewood for them and made them fires in the winter; with a wheelbarrow he went shopping for them in nearby Mutoko. When the lepers were sick he would sit with them, when they were dying he would stay with them all night and when they died he would bury them. Of one of his leper friends, he wrote:

> There is an old lady (called Marchareeda or Matilda) who has no eyes and no hands, and has until this month been feeding herself with her face in her plate much as an animal might. She cannot use a spoon. Of the food she was given, dogs and hens used to steal at least half, and a further quarter would be either spilled or smeared over her face and dress. So now I either feed her myself with a spoon, slowly, or if I am too busy with medical matters I get one of the orderlies to do it. It is great fun feeding her and she thoroughly enjoys it.

Bradburne would start each morning 'round' with a wheelbarrow full of gifts that he had been given to distribute among the lepers; nuts, sweets, tea, vegetables, tomatoes, bread, meat and much else besides. By the time that he returned to his chapel to pray the Angelus at midday, the barrow was empty. Fr Gibbs records:

> After a period of quiet in the presence of the Lord, the afternoon would be spent in much the same way – cutting firewood, cleaning out the cattle grid, collecting reeds for making hats, making tea or coffee for the sick or just popping in to chat and cheer up the people. Once or twice a week John would go up to the village to do the shopping for the lepers.
>
> For those really ill or dying, John would buy something special at the village – perhaps fresh oranges, an egg or two, an extra portion of milk or a pint of 'real' milk. On his return from shopping he would visit his 'special' patients – those seriously ill at the time – and help them to get their fire lit, bed made, pipe filled, coffee boiled or whatever other small tasks needed to be done. Sometimes he would simply crouch on his haunches and chatter away, trying to help and encourage.

The Rosary and evening prayers were said in the church at 4pm, allowing the lepers to gather for their evening meal at 5pm and Bradburne to begin his daily cycle of prayer once more.

In the midst of his labours, poetry flowed incessantly from Bradburne, each of his leper friends being captured in verse. He was able to share much of his poetry with a Jesuit who arrived at Silveira House in 1973, Fr David Harold-

Barry. On one occasion, he clearly instructed Harold-Barry to destroy any of his poems if he thought that they were not in keeping with the faith of the church.

VOCATION FOUND

An early poem from Bradburne's years at Mtemwa expresses his awe and joy at the vocation that he had discovered:

This people, this exotic clan
Of lepers in array
Of being less yet more than man
As man is worn today:
This is a people born to be
Burnt upward to eternity!

This strange ecstatic moody folk
Of joy with sorrow merged
Destined to shuffle off the yoke
Of all the world has urged:
This oddity, this Godward school
Sublimely wise, whence, I'm its fool!

Friends supported his work: the lady with whom he had first gone to Mtemwa inspiring the school where she taught to collect money so that Bradburne could purchase a donkey cart to make the distribution of food and medicine more easily throughout the camp. Others sent gifts of food, clothes and medicine for the lepers, with the occasional bottle of brandy for Bradburne himself. According to his friends:

John went to Mtemwa and, in doing so, experienced a fulfilment. He often used to say to us that he felt he had come 'home'. John's love of his fellow men extended far beyond the bounds of conventional charity. He loved as Jesus loved. To him, the lepers were his family. There was a deep personal relationship. They were Peter, Joshua, Hanzu, to mention only a few.

If he happened to be away from them for a short while, it troubled him. "What if someone has taken ill and needs me?" he would say. He cared for them in the true sense of the word and they, in turn, gave him love and friendship. When we visited John at Mtemwa, we also visited his 'family' and were introduced to them all. One never came away from there without feeling spiritually refreshed.

NEW CHAPEL

The physical care of the lepers was not enough for Bradburne, who provided daily services for the lepers in the dilapidated chapel of the camp. At first a priest came only once a month to say Mass for the lepers. Very soon he was coming every week and, after some time, Bradburne himself was permitted to distribute Holy Communion to the lepers. Just one year after having arrived, Bradburne had a new chapel built. It was designed by a friend to echo the shape of the lepers' huts – a round building with a conical roof. Friends gave a table for an altar, a cloth to be placed upon it, a chalice and a tabernacle for the Blessed Sacrament. Bradburne was overjoyed to have been given a harmonium for the chapel and subsequently spent many hours of his spare time singing as he accompanied himself and teaching the lepers to sing Gregorian chant in Shona as well as popular hymn tunes to which were also set words in Shona.

Despite being so cut off at Mtemwa, Bradburne was able to make new friends. One such was Pauline Hutchings, a lady whose husband, Tony, was a farmer near to Mtemwa. Pauline decided to become a Catholic and Fr Dove directed her to Bradburne for instruction. He was happy to help Pauline and met her once a week until she was received into the Catholic Church. His manner of instruction was different from most as he would not use a catechism, insisting that, "Religion true is rather caught than taught."

Bradburne would simply describe the life of the camp and answer such questions as Pauline put to him. The two became lifelong friends.

Fr John Dove, perhaps the friend who had the deepest insight into John Bradburne's personality, recalled how Bradburne yearned for a solitary life and yet longed to be with people. He was an acutely sensitive man who, "fought down any praise – and he did it vehemently. He seemed terrified of honour or pride and he struggled mightily not to take himself seriously." Others were the extraordinary figures in his world, described by him as, 'colossal', rock-like' or 'serene'. He was, he himself proclaimed, a 'clown', 'an idle fellow', 'a fraud', 'Master Shallow'.

EXILE

In August 1971, Fr Ennis, the Vice-Chairman of the 'Friends of Mtemwa' came to the end of his term of office as Superior of the Jesuit Mission. Both responsibilities were handed over to his successor but, following disagreements with the Friends of Mtemwa committee, that priest resigned. It seems that the dispute came about due to the proposed expansion of the work of the committee and of care of lepers to the whole of Zimbabwe, changing the committee's name to the Rhodesian Leprosy Association in the process. The Jesuit

superior believed that the lepers at Mtemwa were better served by a distinct organisation. With Fr Ennis and his successor no longer on the committee, Bradburne was now less well known and understood. Among the new members of the enlarged committee was a government doctor who regarded Bradburne as a religious 'hippy' and, "perhaps a little mad with an innate fear of responsibility." Despite Bradburne disagreeing with the doctor on a number of issues (Bradburne was against the proposal to introduce family planning, for instance) the two respected each other.

But as the remit of the committee expanded, so did its determination to tighten up administration. Bradburne cared about individuals and hardly at all about desk administration. He was sacked as warden and expelled from the settlement in April 1973 precisely because the committee believed him to be careless with the bookkeeping and too generous with the rations that he was handing out to the lepers. To be sure that he left, two police officers were sent from Mutoko to see him off the premises and to ensure that there was no disorder.

New regulations were introduced to govern the life of Mtemwa – the lepers were to wear number tags around their necks and their rations to be cut. "The lepers need me to stay and keep watch," Bradburne said, and did. Two friends provided him with a tent which he set up on Mount Chigona, a height very near the edge of the leper camp. The lepers themselves cleared a path between the tent and the camp and from the rocky height on which the tent was pitched – the tent being anchored by stones – Bradburne could see every hut in the leper colony. He was still the caretaker of the chapel, so he was allowed to go there, but he only ventured into the camp at night if a leper was particularly sick.

The lepers were concerned for their former warden, worrying that his tent could be blown away by the mini whirlwinds that were common in that area or that he might be attacked by a leopard, so they found him a disused hut very close to the camp itself. At first Bradburne liked the new warden of Mtemwa but the relationship between the two soon broke down as Bradburne took the side of the lepers who came to him to complain about how they were treated by the new regime. By Easter 1974, the Leprosy Association was attempting to have Bradburne evicted from the area and obtained a court injunction banning him from the leper camp but, as the Archdiocesan custodian of the chapel, he clearly had the right to live where he was and enter the chapel himself. A friend of Bradburne recorded the zeal with which Bradburne was determined to keep watch over the lepers:

He retained his old fiery spirit, brilliant wit and carried on with zest a running verbal and written battle with several members of the Rhodesian Leprosy Association. This was exacerbated by the fact that, unlike lesser mortals who out of habit compromise on many things, it never entered John's head to do so. This could be awkward for the person trying to play a diplomatic role. He had no time for this at all – just came out with what he thought was right – and was concerned with being right in terms of his great devotion to, and absorption with, the Word of God.

PIPER'S VALE

Yet, the lepers had to be careful: if they were perceived to be sympathetic to Bradburne, the new warden, they felt, made life more difficult for them. As relations worsened, and care and love for the lepers lessened, a further dispute between the Italian sisters who provided medical care and other kinds of assistance to the camp, caused them to reluctantly leave Mtemwa. It was alleged that the warden had made sexual advances on one of the sisters – Bradburne hearing that others in the camp had suffered in a similar way.

With their diet reduced and rations of fresh fruit being stolen by the warden, the lepers' health soon began to suffer. As Fr John Dove, a regular visitor to the camp noted, "The lepers now had no John, no medical care and above all no love…I noticed the decline in morale."

Meanwhile a kindly local farmer provided Bradburne with a tin hut that Bradburne named Piper's Vale. Bradburne liked the acoustics of the hut for singing his prayers and, after receiving a donation, he was able to build two small brick and thatch guest huts next to it. These huts allowed him to temporarily house lepers who were waiting to be admitted to the camp and those who were evicted from there.

Whilst the Rhodesian Leprosy Association made monthly visits to inspect the camp, the warden was careful to ensure that all appeared to be in order when they came. Bradburne and Fr Dove believed that sometimes the lepers were assaulted but the committee in charge of the camp never accepted any accusation that Bradburne made. They thought him a mad man. Not so the lepers or other friends of Bradburne. One recorded that, whilst warden of the camp, Bradburne:

> …taught the people to sing hymns, say prayers, and to pray the Rosary, but he never did any preaching or general teaching except by his example. Many of the old people depended heavily on him, Peter, for example, a blind and helpless old man whom John bathed and cared for in so many ways. There were others too but he had no sentimental ideas about his role there and never considered himself indispensable to them. In fact he would often extol the lepers for their patience in putting up with him who blew up when they cut down trees, was intolerant of habitual hard drinking, and who often criticised their apparent lack of religious responsibility and fervour.
>
> Sometimes he longed to get away from Mtemwa and return to Jerusalem…. It is true he was occasionally disappointed in the lepers, but his righteous indignation

was overwhelmingly tempered by his sorrow for their physical anguish, his respect for their deep spirituality and his great love for them. He used to say: "If you need to storm Heaven, ask the lepers to pray; their prayers go straight there."

DRAWN BY LOVE

Through the increasing challenges and the rejection that he suffered, Bradburne was sustained by a deep life of prayer that grew from following the rule of the Third Order of St Francis and its stipulation that members of the Third Order should daily recite the Little Office of the Blessed Virgin, which he usually sang. The Mass, daily reception of Holy Communion and reading from the Bible were essential for him. He also cherished his copy of the *Cloud of Unknowing*, in which Fr John Dove noted that Bradburne had underlined short passages:

> Unite yourself to Him by love and trust, and by that union you will be joined both to Him and to all who like yourself are united by love to Him – with Our Lady St Mary…
>
> Strike that thick cloud of unknowing with the sharp dart of longing love, and on no account whatever think of giving up.
>
> …you should have this blind out-reaching love to God himself, this secret love pressing upon the cloud of unknowing.

Fr Dove, citing the *Cloud* in his biography of Bradburne, drew a clear parallel between its assertion that "God may be well-loved but not thought. By love He can be thought and held, but by thinking never," and John's spiritual life:

One noticed this aspect very much in John – he was drawn by love. He was not a Pelagian-muscular Christian who drew himself up to God by the sheer weight of his penances, self denials and studied practice of the virtues.

The exciting thing about John was that he was in a sense unmortified, he would let go, but he was always drawn back on to the path up to God by love. He was brought to sanctity, if one may use the term, not by hard discipline but by his longing, his love for God. One might say that John's big-hearted love covered a multitude of sins. The Lord left him with enough 'failings' to keep him humble – pride, anger, passion – all of which, incidentally, were used in defence of the lepers.

He was a lover 'par excellence' and God brought him to that final act of supreme love when he died for his little flock. It is all so encouraging since he was never the bolt-upright 'saint' (if such a one ever existed).

Bradburne lived, however, a life that would make lesser mortals blanch. Not only were his nocturnal prayers and vigils by the dying demanding but even more so was the sheer lack of facilities for washing and a regular toilet, let alone the heat that must have built up in his tin hut. Furthermore he lived close to an area where mosquitos were breeding and his diet was minimal.

Given the authenticity of his life of prayer and poverty, a friend of Bradburne, Fr Seán Gildea OFM, Superior of the Franciscans in Zimbabwe, arranged for Fr Dove to officially clothe Bradburne in the Franciscan habit. Fr Gildea would often say that John Bradburne was, "more Franciscan than the whole lot of us put together."

"I gave John the Franciscan habit," Fr Gildea wrote, "because he was living a Franciscan life, was committed to St Francis and made the values of St Francis present; prayer, love, poverty, generosity, joy, deep faith […] I could go on."

Not being able to find the ritual prayer for the ceremony of clothing, Fr Dove adapted a prayer for the blessing of a processional banner. Fr Dove did not keep an exact copy of the words that he used but later recorded a version of the prayer as best he could remember it:

Lord Jesus Christ whose church is like an army set in battle array, bless this habit so that he who wears it in the name of the Lord God of Hosts, may through the intercession of St Francis of Assisi be helped to overcome in this life his enemies, visible and invisible, and after victory to triumph in Heaven.

Apparently John Bradburne loved this prayer and particularly appreciated the reference to the troubles he was undergoing at Mtemwa – undoubtedly he felt strengthened by the prayer and affirmed in his vocation by being clothed in the Franciscan habit.

THE CLOUDS OF WAR

In the war for independence, neutrality was not an option, especially for anyone who was in any way perceived as a leader in a community. Bradburne's personal experience of war made him very aware of the violence and destruction that was part and parcel of conflict, and this he hated. But he also loathed the oppression of people by unjust regimes, be they local or more national in scale. He simply wanted to be left alone to continue his mission of care. But the clouds of war were gathering around him by June 1976. A close friend was arrested and imprisoned for allegedly giving medical treatment to a guerrilla. She was released but the war was advancing closer to Salisbury, as it was then, the Rhodesian Security Forces burning villages and their granaries, beating and executing those who were believed to support the guerrillas.

The guerrillas were supported by village boys – called mujhibhas – who reported back to them the movements of the Rhodesian soldiers and the presence of any strangers in the villages or anyone that they were suspicious of. Having gained the trust of the guerrillas, the mujhibhas were given weapons and were sent to source supplies such as food, weapons and petrol. At the same time, the Rhodesian Security Forces were also developing networks to gather information. The very poorest were caught in the crossfire of the war.

As the war for independence advanced, there was relief for Bradburne with regard to his war with the Leprosy Association Committee. Alistair Guthrie, who had visited Bradburne every month for many years, became a member of the committee and gradually persuaded the other members to agree to letting Bradburne accompany him on his visits to the camp. Unexpectedly, in 1977, the warden of Mtemwa was fired, access to the camp being made less stressful for Bradburne. A visitor to the camp at this time was shocked by the sight of the virtually naked lepers 'crawling' on the stumps of their elbows and knees. Bradburne was once again able to care for the lepers in the way that he wanted but this time without the worry of administration as a local villager was employed to deal with this work.

Bradburne's prayer at this time was greatly influenced by a book, *The Way of a Pilgrim*, given to him by a visiting Jesuit priest. The book was by a Russian mystic and encouraged the use of the Jesus prayer. The simplicity of this prayer – "Lord Jesus Christ, Son of God, have mercy on me, a sinner", along with the style of praying it (breathing in before the first part and exhaling for the final words) was immensely attractive to Bradburne. He adapted it to his own personal devotion, praying, "Jesus of Nazareth, King of the Jews, triumph through Judah." Under a mango tree Bradburne would sit, reciting thousands of times a day these words. He said that doing this was, "a good cloud of forgetting to prepare the way for the cloud of unknowing."

In August 1978, Bradburne fell ill from a type of polio virus, encephalitis, which caused him to be semi-paralysed on one side of his face. The disease advanced and he was admitted into intensive care. Gradually he recovered, returning to Mtemwa in October. By this time the area around Mtemwa was very dangerous. Seven Jesuits were gunned down and the safest way to get to the camp was only to be part of a daily convoy of vehicles from Mutoko.

In July 1979, a great friend of Bradburne, Dr Luisa Guidotti, who for years cared for the sick in a nearby mission, bled to death after being shot in the leg whilst driving an ambulance. Throughout Luisa's funeral Mass, Bradburne knelt close to her coffin, acting as one of her pall bearers at the beginning and end of the Mass. After this bereavement a friend, Heather, noticed a transformation in Bradburne:

John was quieter and more serene than I had ever known him. A peace which I was quite unable to share. He was quiet and gentle and talked of God's love, continuously stressing the trust and faith that was possible if one accepted the completeness of God's love. I realised that John understood and embraced, with serene joy and understanding, this love.

With some sense of surprise I perceived that John the 'Joker' – John self-acclaimed 'God's fool', was gone. In his place was a very holy man who, through his life of prayer and meditation, had reached some higher level of understanding.

WHAT SHALL I DO?

At the end of their last conversation, Bradburne asked Fr Dove, "What shall I do if they come?" meaning either mujhibhas or guerrillas. Fr Dove responded by saying that he should give them what they wanted saying, "Don't die for five dollars." "Ah no," retorted Bradburne, "it is leper money. I will give them coffee." Bradburne then knelt down and asked his friend's blessing – they were never to meet again.

THE STORM

By the summer of 1979 the war was everywhere around Mtemwa. There had been a guerrilla attack close to the settlement but the combatants had passed by the camp. But direct attack was often the result of rumours and malicious intent. The war for liberation was, like most wars, an opportunity for evil to thrive with false allegations and old enmities settled, often resulting in the loss of life.

Bradburne was caught up in this diabolical storm. Neighbouring villages that had long disliked the presence of the lepers near them and despised the community of the diseased, many of whom were labourers from abroad or from different tribes from those in the locality, did not miss their opportunity to voice their complaints, casting suspicion on Bradburne, the white Englishman who, for no obvious reason, was a fierce defender of the lepers. These hostile voices noted the antagonism that Bradburne had for the African warden who was sacked. They disdained him for condemning some of the villagers for murdering an elderly man who attended Mass at Mtemwa, and for the constant pillaging of fruit and other commodities from the camp.

With the appointment of a new warden, the illicit supply of stolen goods from the camp to some locals was stopped, Bradburne being held responsible for this by those now worse off. He was unpopular with some for constantly struggling to keep villagers' cattle out of the camp's graveyard. It was known that Bradburne had some kind of electronic device (it was simply a radio) and it was alleged that this was actually a transmitter which he used to inform the Rhodesian authorities of their enemies' movements. Bradburne was also suspected by the Rhodesian forces of collaborating with the guerrillas – how else had he survived? Resentment and grudges against the Englishman were ever-increasing. In such an atmosphere the lives of most missionaries, members of the Red Cross and foreign medical men and women were very vulnerable and many were murdered.

With tension rising daily, military helicopters often hovering overhead, Bradburne decided to move into the middle hut of the three that he had – a round brick hut with a thatched roof and a few small holes in the walls, rather than windows. It was cooler but darker and certainly safer. Bradburne clearly sensed danger, moving from the hut for a couple of nights to stay in the chapel instead.

Indeed, according to friends, Bradburne was clearly aware that should he stay at Mtemwa, it was more than likely that he might be killed: "He knew there was a good possibility that he should be killed," wrote one friend, "and it was the culmination of his offering."

His brother, Philip, wrote to him, expressing the worry of all his family, asking him to leave Mtemwa. To Bradburne, the possibility that he might be harmed mattered less to him than the horror of abandoning his leper family. As Bradburne said to a friend:

> You see, I love these people. Maybe it is a selfish love, because before I met these people, I did not feel I loved anyone, but the day I got in contact with these people, I felt I loved somebody, I felt that at last I contributed something to some people who appreciated it. And this way I really love these people.

CHAPTER 6

No Greater Love

On Sunday 2nd September 1979, Bradburne held a service of Holy Communion, as no priest was available to come to say Mass in the camp. He preached on the life of the early Christian martyr, St Lawrence, even though it was not the saint's feast day, holding the saint up as an example of Christian courage and perseverance, even in the face of death. When the third-century deacon heard his persecutors demand that he present to them the treasures of the church, St Lawrence gestured to the poor, the sick and the crippled saying that they were the treasures of the church.

No wonder that John Bradburne was inspired by St Lawrence's final act of defiance to the forces of evil. Fr Dove remembered that Bradburne often would quote lines from the prophet Jeremiah:

> But you, dress yourself for work; arise, and say to them everything that I command you. Do not be dismayed by them, lest I dismay you before them. And I, behold, I make you this day a fortified city, an iron pillar, and bronze walls, against the whole land, against the kings of Judah, its officials, its priests, and the people of the land. (*Jr* 1:17)

Around midnight of that Sunday Bradburne heard a group of ten to fifteen men banging on the door of the thatched hut where he was sleeping. The men, armed with sticks and hoes, were demanding that Bradburne come out of the hut to pray with them. Bradburne put on his Franciscan habit and red hairband and reluctantly opened the door. He was led away, the captors still using the pretence that they wanted to pray with him. He was led into the bush where his hands were tied and he began to protest saying, "Is this the way you ask me to pray?"

For over six miles from Mtemwa he was marched until the group arrived at Chimedza Cave near Hunhu village. The cave was a stronghold for over thirty mujhibhas who began to subject Bradburne to mockery, threatened him with the idea that he might be forced to eat faeces, attempting to make him dance, and trying to force him to have sex with a village girl, both of which he firmly refused to do.

As day began to dawn, Bradburne's hands were again tied and he was led off to a nearby village where he was imprisoned in an empty hut. Leading members of the local Zanu PF (Zimbabwe African National Union – Patriotic Front) were assembled but they testified to Bradburne's good work for the lepers. The mujhibhas said that they would release him – a blatant lie. And so on the night of 3rd September, Bradburne was frogmarched to a nearby cave that was under a different commander to the Chimedza Cave. They arrived at Gwaze Cave at dawn on Tuesday 4th September. Bradburne immediately saw a rock painting of the figure of Christ with his arms outstretched. He knelt before the image in silent prayer, utterly exhausted.

When the district commander of the guerrillas arrived at Gwaze, he wanted to know why Bradburne had been brought. The mujhibhas response – that Bradburne was not helping them in their armed struggle for freedom and that he didn't pray to the ancestral spirits – infuriated the commander. He saw the whole episode of Bradburne being brought to their Gwaze hideout as potentially disastrous if they had been followed. The commander ordered that Bradburne be freed and sent back to Mtemwa. But the officer in the guerrilla group in charge of security disagreed with this decision, saying that Bradburne had seen too much and that the Rhodesian Security Forces might interrogate him to extract information about the guerrillas and their command posts.

After virulent arguing one way and the other, it was decided that Bradburne be sent out of the way to Mozambique, but their captive refused to go anywhere but back to his 'family' of lepers at Mtemwa. When questioned as to whether or not he supported the freedom fight, Bradburne's only response was to kneel and pray the Our Father and Hail Mary in Shona. The commander still wanted to release Bradburne and took him, along with his men, to a gathering of local villagers, after which Bradburne was told that he was to be released.

Bradburne walked with villagers in the direction of the main road to Mutoko. Some of the villagers noticed that Bradburne stopped twice to pray – they were also disturbed by the presence of two guerrillas armed with Kalashnikovs, not understanding why they were needed if Bradburne had indeed been released.

After the villagers and Bradburne had reached the main Mutoko-Nyamapanda road, one of the gunmen took John Bradburne by the arm and led him towards a little stream. Bradburne knelt to pray. As he stood, the gunman fired a round of bullets into Bradburne's back. He fell on his knees and, according to a witness, silently died.

THE SOUND OF SINGING

The group was horrified, not least because they feared that should Bradburne's body be discovered by the white security forces, the inhabitants of the villages around about

JOHN BRADBURNE
SERVANT OF GOD

1921 — 1979
(2013)

could face a deadly revenge. The plan was hatched that the group would carry Bradburne's body back over the main road and hide it in the rocky terrain. A witness relates that as the group began to carry the body across the road they were startled by the sound of singing. Terrified, they dropped Bradburne's body until they had regained their nerves and attempted to move it again. But the singing, and this time louder and clearer, started once more and once again the villagers fled.

Their fear of the security forces was, however, greater than their fear of the inexplicable singing and so the villagers returned again to Bradburne's body. Fr John Dove relates the account of what happened next:

> …they saw something never seen before. A strange, large white bird hovered over John's body. It moved up and down over the body seeming to guard it. They retreated again in alarm, but they were torn between fear of these phenomena and fear of the security forces. They lay low for quite a while and then plucked up the courage to go back to the road for a third time.
>
> They were overawed on arrival at the sight of what appeared to be three beams of light ascending from the proximity of John's body, meeting at a height and descending as one beam. The colours seemed to be blue, red and white. They fled, not to return again.

Fr Dove continues his account by interpreting the experiences that the villagers encountered in the light of John Bradburne's life:

> Voices singing? – how John longed to hear the choirs of Heaven. A very large white bird – the Holy Spirit? Finally three beams of light joining and forming one. John so loved the Holy Trinity.

The villager who recounted these phenomena was an old man who honoured ancestral spirits, he was not a Christian, and thus in no way inclined to create a hagiographical account of the phenomena around John Bradburne's body. The old man was simply as terrified as the rest of the group and related what he heard and saw.

Bradburne's body was therefore not hidden but left at the edge of the deserted road where it was found the following day by Fr David Gibbs. Fr Gibbs observed that John Bradburne's almost naked body had wounds in the lower part of his chest and his legs. The body had been left lying on his back – Fr Gibbs closed Bradburne's eyes and, after briefly praying, moved the body to the mission ambulance that he had driven to the scene, taking the remains to the Military Joint Operations Command in Mutoko, where Fr Gibbs knew that there was a fridge capable of keeping human bodies.

FUNERAL

The 10th September was chosen as the date for John Bradburne's funeral at the Cathedral of the Sacred Heart, Harare, the celebrant being Archbishop Patrick Chakaipa. The Anglican Bishop of Salisbury also was to attend. The music chosen was that which John Bradburne loved including Pachelbel's *Canon in D* as his coffin was borne into the cathedral, Gregorian chant sung in Shona and Mozart's *Ave Verum*.

The readings chosen for the funeral poignantly reminded the congregation of his character. The first reading was taken from Isaiah 58:6:

Is not this the fast that I choose:
to loose the bonds of wickedness,
to undo the thongs of the yoke,
to let the oppressed go free,
and to break every yoke?
Is it not to share your bread with the hungry,
and bring the homeless poor into your house;
when you see the naked, to cover him,
and not to hide yourself from your own flesh?
Then shall your light break forth like the dawn,
and your healing shall spring up speedily;
your righteousness shall go before you,
the glory of the Lord shall be your rear guard.
Then you shall call, and the Lord will answer;
you shall cry, and he will say, "Here I am."

The second reading was Acts 3, St Peter curing the crippled man by the Beautiful Gate in Jerusalem, saying that though he had not silver or gold, in the name of Jesus Christ of Nazareth, the man was to get up and walk.

The Gospel read was the account of Jesus in the synagogue at Nazareth where he read from the prophet Isaiah's words:

> The Spirit of the Lord is upon me,
> because he has anointed me to proclaim good news to the poor.
> He has sent me to proclaim release to the captives
> and recovering of sight to the blind,
> to set at liberty those who are oppressed,
> to proclaim the year of the Lord's favour. (*Lk* 4:18)

The Lord's concluding remark, made as he gave the scroll back to the synagogue attendant, must have seemed particularly apposite as the congregation reflected on John Bradburne's life: "Today this scripture has been fulfilled in your hearing."

The funeral homily was given by Fr Harold-Barry. He recalled how Bradburne seemed, "always with a twinkle in his eye and always seeming to live without effort and constantly full of joy," noting that, "we were somehow tempted to think that it was easy for him that life for him was just a long, peaceful river." Yet, he continued:

> We know that what John became was the flower and fruit of much inner silent generosity. Was it an easy thing to

travel as he did with next to no money or provisions? Was it easy to live in a hut for so many years with little food and no running water? Was it so easy for him to live alongside the lepers and belong to them? Was it so easy for him to spend long hours in prayer?

Do we not catch ourselves saying: 'but he loved that life.' Yes, he did. But let us be sure to remember that his life was a triumph of a generous response to God's love. Sure, God makes the road easy – for such generous people – and the burden light. But let us be very certain that there was a generous inner silent discipline in John. This is why I say John shows us the hidden life of Jesus. He chose a very clear manifestation of that hiddenness. We come today to show our sorrow, yes, but to show our joy too at having known John. Let us flesh out that knowledge in this way: by treasuring the hidden life of Jesus.

DROPS OF BLOOD

During the time of Holy Communion three lilies were laid on Bradburne's casket at the request of a close friend. As the flowers were placed, three drops of blood appeared on the floor underneath the coffin. The lady who placed the flowers later recounted that as she did so she felt as though she had been caught up in a "spiritual whirlpool". A number of people nearby saw the blood dripping three times from the coffin and a Jesuit priest took care to preserve it on a purificator that he placed on the floor.

This totally unexpected happening caused the coffin to be reopened after the funeral Mass, having been returned to the funeral parlour. As when they had first received the body, the undertakers noted its perfect preservation and there was no sign at all of blood in the coffin. The possibility of bleeding from a body of someone who had been dead for five days was also totally beyond the undertaker's imagining.

It was at this time that it was realised that John Bradburne's body had not been clothed in the Franciscan habit as he had wished. A habit was procured and the body duly clothed in it. Burial was to have taken place at Mtemwa but, as the region was unsafe, John Bradburne was buried at the Chishawasha Mission, close to the graves of the Dominican sisters, Jesuit priests and brothers who had been killed during the war. John Bradburne's grave immediately became a shrine: rosaries were left hanging on the cross that bore his name and the earth of the grave had to be replenished as the devout took away small amounts of it as relics.

EFFULGENCE OF SANCTITY

During the following years, John Bradburne's reputation of being a holy man steadily increased. In 1980, accounts began to be assembled to form a biography and in 1983 Fr John Dove published his own testimony to his friend, *Strange Vagabond of God: the story of John Bradburne.* Many articles have been written about Bradburne and some documentaries made. In 1995 the John Bradburne Memorial Society was established in Britain.

More significantly, since John Bradburne's death men and women throughout the world believe that they, or their loved ones, received cures from various illnesses through his intercession, cancer cures being the most numerous. The best documented case of the answer to prayers through the intercession of John Bradburne is the cure of William Hamilton in Edinburgh in May 1994.

Hamilton was suffering from a benign brain tumour and had prayed for healing through John Bradburne's intercession. But when the day came for the operation to take place, it was cancelled as the tumour had disappeared. The professor examining Hamilton later wrote, "I think that it is fair to say that his cure was certainly miraculous and may indeed have been due to the prayers and to his faith."

A further sign of the effulgence of John Bradburne's sanctity is the annual pilgrimage to his grave that spontaneously flowered among the people of Zimbabwe. In 1999, fifteen thousand pilgrims were present for the twentieth anniversary of Bradburne's death and, on 1st July of that year the Congregation for the Causes of Saints, the Roman dicastery charged with investigating the lives of those being considered for canonisation, gave permission for the cause of John Bradburne to proceed, Bradburne from then on being acknowledged as a Servant of God.

In 1952 he had written to his friend, John Dove, "Pray on for my sanctification too, because it would encourage so many souls if such a wreckage might come to canonisation, I do so want to by-pass Purgatory!" Many souls are indeed encouraged by seeing how the seeming messiness of Bradburne's life found resolution in his realisation of God's love for him, his love for God and his finding wholeness in his dedication to the lepers whom he loved.

The man who travelled so far from his birthplace found the kingdom of God within. How else did Bradburne articulate this but in verse:

Strange vagabond that knows not what to seek!
The rest you lack lies not this far afield:
Much babel tumult makes your hearing weak,
And all replete with sights your eyes are sealed.
Far out you've strayed to find your inmost soul
But souls their eloquence in stillness find:
Be still then! Let God's silence make you whole,
For He alone can calm your troubled mind.

Your heart's desire is nearest, though unseen,
Your haven of perfection close at hand;
And that drear quest was a fevered dream;
God's love within you is your native land.
So search none other, never more depart,
For you are homeless, save God keeps your heart.

A PRAYER FOR THE UNIVERSAL RECOGNITION OF THE SERVANT OF GOD JOHN RANDAL BRADBURNE

O Most Holy Trinity, Father, Son and Holy Spirit, we adore You profoundly. You chose John to be a witness of Your Love for the poor and unwanted. You inspired him with a knowledge and love of the true faith. You gave him a great understanding of the mystery of Your own life, as well as an extraordinary love for Mary, Your Mother, which gave him the desire to spread Your Love everywhere.

Knowing that if we ask the Father for anything in the name of His Son, Jesus, He will grant it, we humbly ask that John's virtuous life will be recognised and that he will be declared 'Blessed', by the present Holy Father.

We also pray for a special favour through his prayer and the intercession of Mary our Mother that…

… And if that which I ask is not in conformity with God's Glory and the greater good of my soul, be pleased to grant me what will secure the attainment of both. Amen.

Our Father… Hail Mary… Glory be…

NOVENA PRAYER FOR THE INTRODUCTION OF THE CAUSE OF JOHN RANDAL BRADBURNE

Heavenly Father, You led your humble servant, John Bradburne, along the various paths, guiding him to accept the faith taught by the Catholic Church, and finally through the inspiration of the Holy Spirit, to devote the last ten years of his life to the care of the lepers at Mtemwa in Zimbabwe.

You rewarded his lifelong search for God, by granting him his three wishes. You showed him your special Fatherly Love by granting him a deep understanding of the mystery of Your own divine life. You endowed him with an extraordinary love for Mary, the Mother of Your Son, Who gave Her to us as our Mother, at the foot of the Cross. Love for the Passion of Your Son was seen in his devotion to the Mass, and in his union with Christ in the Blessed Sacrament. His love for Mary was shown by the daily recitation of the Rosary, and in saying or singing Her Office.

We thank You for granting him these favours, and we humbly pray that one day he will be recognised for his virtuous life, and will be declared Venerable by the present Holy Father.

John is an example of self-sacrificing love for the poor and unwanted. Zimbabwe needs a Saint to intercede for the needs of its people and for the salvation of the country.

We thank You, Heavenly Father, because it pleased You to grant him his wish to work with the lepers, a life which was crowned by granting him his second wish in choosing to die rather than to abandon them. His third request was granted after his death, through an incident which was understood to be the sign of Your own personal love for Your humble servant, and those he cared for.

O Mary Immaculate, hear our prayer and grant our petition. Amen.

Our Father… Hail Mary… Glory be…

FURTHER READING

John Dove, *Strange Vagabond of God – The Story of John Bradburne*, published by Gracewing Ltd, 1997.

Didier Rance, *John Bradburne – The Vagabond of God*, published by DLT, 2017.

IMAGES

© **John Bradburne Memorial Society:** pages **3:** John Bradburne; **6:** portrait of John Bradburne; **9:** Bradburne family; **11:** John and his sister; **12:** John (left) with his siblings Mary, Philip and Audrey; **14:** John in the army; **15:** John (second from the right) in the army; **21:** John Dove and John Bradburne, India 1942; **24:** portrait of John Bradburne; **35:** Thomas William Bradburne, John's father; **41:** John playing the recorder; **48:** Fr John Dove and John Bradburne; **55:** Fr John Dove, Fr Brennan, John Bradburne and Fr Hannah at Silveira House; **64, 65, 67, 73, 89:** Mtemwa Leper Camp; **79:** John praying; **88:** John in Zimbabwe; **93:** John Bradburne memorial.

7: Mount Harare in Mutoko, Zimbabwe, Denny-Muta | Shutterstock.com; **25:** Rolling hills of Devon, Lorraine Dixon | Shutterstock.com; **49:** Rock formations of the Matopos National Park, Zimbabwe, Vladislav T. Jirousek | Shutterstock.com.